NATURE

Gallery Edition

Illustrated Poems

Part 2

By

William Fontana Sr.

Edited and Cover Designed By

William Fontana Jr.

ISBN-13: 978-0692212363 (Fontana-Art.com)

ISBN-10: 0692212361

Introduction

As with all things human, there should be a reason or motive. Mine is very simple: *I want the world to continue!* If, some years ago, someone would have said to me, "Bill, you are going to be a writer," I would have simply thought they were dreadfully wrong. But here I am, writing away. I hope that you enjoy these poems and pictures. I also hope that *they lift your spirit, strengthen your soul and enhance your nature vision.*

Table of Contents

Energy	pgs.	5-6
The Portal to Pure Wilderness	pgs.	7-8
Raven	pgs.	9-11
Yosemite Falls	pgs.	12-13
Moon over Half Dome	pgs.	14-15
Excommunication	pgs.	16-17
Nature's Fragments	pgs.	18-19
Circles	pgs.	20-21
The Natives	pgs.	22-23
Remnants	pgs.	24-25
Aggression	pgs.	26-27
Attention	pgs.	28-29
Salute	pgs.	30-31
Velocity	pgs.	32-33
Consciousness	pgs.	34-36
Awareness	pgs.	37-38
The Unconscious	pgs.	39-40
Wilderness	pgs.	41-42
The Portal to Pure Wilderness	pgs.	41-42
All of the Best	pgs.	43-44
The Pool of Love	pgs.	45-46

Poetry	pgs.	47-48
Evolution or Creation	pgs.	49-50
The Company Lawyer	pgs.	51-52
Light and Shadow	pgs.	53-54
Nymphs, Fairies, Elves, Leprechauns, Sprites	pgs.	55-56
Meadow	pgs.	57-58
Speaking Up for the Dead	pgs.	59-60
The Poet Paul Rivers	pgs.	61-63
Writer	pgs.	64-65
Trees	pgs.	66
Efficiency	pgs,	67-68
Light	pgs.	69-70
Flight of the Eagle	pgs.	71-72
Field Mouse	pgs.	73-74
Master Fisherman Ron Silva (Ras)	pgs.	75-77
Transparency	pgs.	78-79
Polity	pgs.	80-81
Spinning and Weaving	pgs.	82-83
Equations	pgs.	84-85
Love	pgs.	86-87
Rainbow	pgs.	88-89
Snow	pgs.	90-91
Salamander	pgs.	92-93
Fox	pgs.	94-95
Mountain Lion	pgs.	95-96

Lone Wolf	pgs.	97-98
Dream	pgs.	99-100
Resurrection	pgs.	101-102
Cosmos	pgs.	103-104
Positive Change	pgs.	105-107
Layers	pgs.	108-109
Image Credits	pgs.	110

Energy

Energy stored in the red of the dogwood leaves.

Energy stored in the snowpack.

Energy released by the waterfalls.

Energy used by the plants and animals as they live and grow.

But cosmic energy is something else.

I can feel the energy concentration starting in the late summer.

The focused energy of winter gives me the strength to create.

The abundant energy of summer is celebrated by the plants and animals.

At the summer solstice, the energy cycle is reloaded, to be used again.

With the nature vortex there is another kind of energy.

Here one must always acknowledge the ultimate power of nature.

One must tread lightly, surrounded by unseen powers.

We must begin to see things differently.

You might say we must look through the tree rather than at it.

We must develop our *nature vision*.

We must be humble in the face of nature,

 Or lose our energy that comes from nature.

The Portal to Pure Wilderness

There are many portals in life.

Some are physical and some are spiritual.

When we think of wilderness,

Are we bothered by impurity?

A butterfly hit by a speeding car,

A wolf caught in a leg hold trap,

Salmon being caught in Alaska to be shipped to Australia,

And ten thousand cars in Yosemite Valley on a summers day!

Is there a portal to the pure wilderness?

I do believe there is.

What does it look like?

Where is it?

Raven

You landed right there.

You tilted your head to the right and then to the left,

Touched your beak to the ground,

Cawed three times.

I look at you and wonder.

How old are your kind?

How much do you know?

The black of your feathers holds all color.

The streamlined shape of your body holds all potential.

Your velocity is something that I can hardly dream of.

You seem to be trying to tell me something

I cannot understand.

You see something I cannot see.

Can you tell me about it?

When you fly with your magnificent symmetrical wings outstretched,

I see a flash of something divine

That only your wings can reach.

When is it that you feel it?

When you are flying full out?

When you are diving or tumbling in free fall?

When is it that you leave us so far behind?

Yosemite Falls

John Muir spoke of shooting comets,

Thomas Starr King of emeralds and light,

Both were right.

Each droplet is a diamond of light.

Each droplet is a potential life.

As they cascade in spinning splendor,

They hold more than light,

They hold more than life.

They are a window to something dimly seen.

They are an individual mirror.

They are a diamond of incomprehensible facets.

They dance, spin, and sing in erotic delight.

Life, hope, and cosmic eternity celebrated.

Moon Over Half Dome

Ansell Adams celebrated the moon over Half Dome.

The moon over Half Dome fills the air with magic;

In the gossamer ephemeral light,

Spirits dance and play.

When the moon is half,

The souls of the dead travel;

When the moon is three-quarters, the love spirits dance;

When the moon is full one mind cannot behold the scope of its touch,

The moonlight on the shimmering water

The way it lays with the leaves of the trees,

Sings to the sleeping birds,

Touches the closed butterfly wings,

And opens the evening primrose.

Excommunication

How long ago was it that we stopped communicating with the animals?

Was it two thousand years ago or two hundred thousand years ago?

Who knows?

Who cares?

Did we stop because we went a different way?

Did we stop because we became too arrogant?

Was it our digits, or was it our brain size?

Do they want to talk anymore?

But if they do how can we ever explain what we have done?

How can we justify the way we have used them, killed them, and made them suffer?

Nature's Fragments

What was it that I just saw?

Was it there or just my imagination?

Another fragment went flitting by.

A broken twig.

A blue feather.

Autumn leaves with the sunlight behind,

The little duck showing me how wonderful her watery world is,

The raven with its symmetrical flight,

A trout swims in

The emerald green water,

flowing by the delightful rocks and sand.

Half Dome and Sentinel Rock,

Yosemite Falls.

All fragments that when taken together,

Stand for something else.

Circles

What can I add to what Ralph Waldo Emerson has written?

I saw today, as I swam in the Merced River, Emerson's circles,

Illuminated below me in the water on the rocks,

Each circle, encompassed by its predecessor,

Yes, they reminded me of that great essay,

Circles within circles, no ending and no beginning.

Will they be circles of intellect that will tear down the old to build a new reality?

Will they be a new political order?

Or will they be from a small child who drops a pebble in the Merced River?

Could that little hand and that little pebble start the all-encompassing circle?

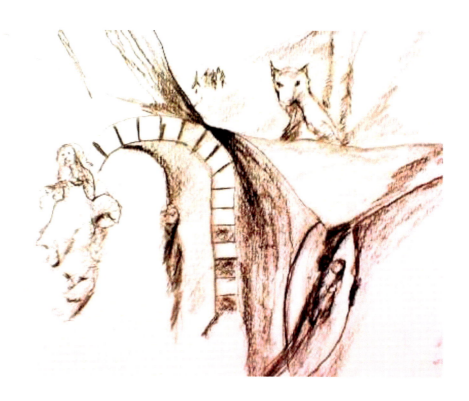

The Natives

Their ways are subdued now.

The meadow wetlands are dry now.

The oak trees are dying now.

No longer do they hunt and dance freely.

No longer do they speak their native tongue.

Their ways and their power were victims of the Gold Rush.

But the Gold Rush never ended.

The cars enter Yosemite Valley by the thousands now.

Nature's temple has become a parking lot.

I know some of them, they are my friends.

And for a fleeting moment,

They can bring back the past,

But, only for a moment

Julia Parker, when she shows the children her basket making skill.

Ben Cunningham-Summerfield, when he plays his flute.

Phillip Johnson, when he, with his soft smile, inducts kids into the Miwok tribe.

If only we could see how it was.

If only we could go back,

To some of that wild meadowland harmony,

The harmony that we can feel when Ben plays his flute,

How much gold would that be worth?

Remnants

Here in Yosemite we live in the land of remnants.

Remnants of the glaciers,

Remnants of the Native Americans,

Remnants of the giant sequoias,

Remnants of the black oak woodlands,

Remnants of the large beautiful valley meadows,

Remnants of the Hetch Hetchy Valley,

Remnants of John Muir, Galen Clark, and Reverend Thomas Starr King,

Remnants of the whole Victorian age,

Remnants of the beautiful golden grizzly bear.

When one picks up a remnant

And turns it slowly in their mind,

One should ask,

How did this item become a remnant?

What does its remnant status signify?

Is its relegation to remnant status a good thing or a bad thing?

What role did we play in making this a remnant?

Could we possibly use this remnant to find a way back to its time?

Maybe we should be more careful with remnants.

Maybe we should try to understand them better.

After all, someday we will all be remnants as well,

And when we become remnants,

Will who or whatever gazes upon our remnants be as glib about them as we are?

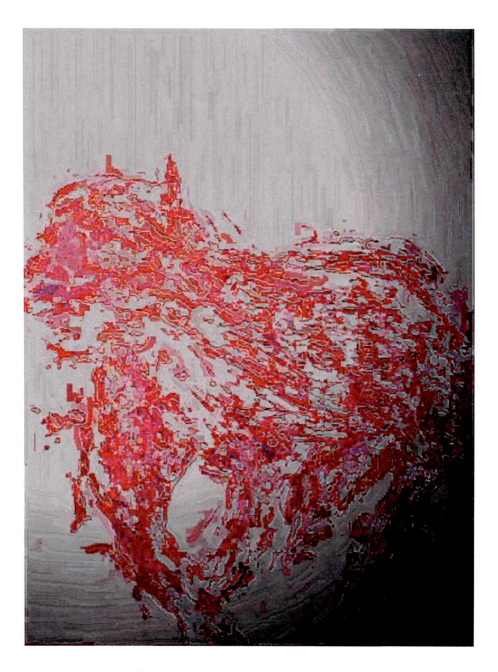

Aggression

They are all very aggressive in their three dimensional world.

The grey squirrel flies in the tree branches over a hundred feet off of the ground.

The ground squirrel makes large tunnels through rocky soil.

The monarch butterfly migrates for thousands of miles.

The acorn woodpecker hollows storage holes in the sides of the oaks.

The raven flies like the wind and dives in carefree abandon.

The bear tears apart trees for grubs.

And the little river duck is constantly moving and searching for food.

They all aggressively seize each day's spatial opportunity.

They aggressively fight, kill, flee, play, forage, and pursue.

They are wild creatures who know that to give up on aggression in their three dimensional world,

Means death.

They aggressively celebrate and revel with less abstraction.

The digital world like a siren beckons the children today.

While it educates, teaches, and empowers them,

It also seduces and makes them passive.

What would the fox, duck or raven say about getting lost in the digital world?

Is there something they know about the value of living with less abstraction

That they are not telling us?

Attention

Are you paying attention?

The art of attention is to the craft.

Women pay attention to women's craft.

Men pay attention to men's craft.

The raven to raven's craft.

The duck to water's craft.

For every living thing, there is a craft that they must attend to.

It is cross-craft attention that is so interesting.

When a woman pays attention to coyote's craft,

Or a child to butterfly craft,

Our lives are crafted by the attention.

Divergence comes from attention to a specific part of nature's craft.

Unity comes from paying attention to the whole of nature's craft.

Salute

How important is the salute!

You salute and become one in purpose.

You feel fraternity.

You feel power.

You dampen alienation.

So it is important that we always recognize a well-intended salute.

The ravens are the best at saluting.

They fly in salute,

They vocally salute,

And they salute while standing.

We really should recognize and acknowledge well-intended animal salutes.

Why do they salute us?

And why don't we salute them?

Velocity

Is my velocity the same as a hare?

Or an eagle?

Or a dog?

How about a snake or lizard?

A whale?

How fast am I moving not relative to the cosmos,

But relative to other living things?

I do not believe that we understand planar velocity.

Life planes of velocity.

Living things travel at different velocities.

While we are in one consistent time frame,

They are in another.

If we could fly with crows,

Swim with whales,

Trot with the fox,

We might understand relative velocity better.

Consciousness

When I am dreaming,

I believe I am conscious.

When I am awake,

I believe I am conscious.

There must be a way to tell

If we are really conscious.

Of course that assumes that there is a true conscious state.

That is what bothers me the most.

I want to be conscious,

But are we ever conscious?

To believe we are conscious proves nothing.

There are reassuring signs of consciousness.

When we are cut, we hurt.

When we swim, we can feel the water.

We can study our fingers to make sure they are there and real.

If they are real we can write with them.

We are reassured by the call of the flicker,

Or the color of its feathers.

Only in nature do we see a reassuring complexity.

But could it also be that complexity in nature and consciousness are the same?

When we simplify our dimensionality from three to two,

When we look for the answers to medicine in single molecules,

When we isolate ourselves from nature in artificial environments,

When we cause extinction of other living creatures,

When we pay attention to war craft,

When we use chemicals to modify our soil for improved farm yields,

When we follow formulaic plots in our movies,

When we, in so many ways,

Strive to work against the complexity of nature,

Are we losing consciousness?

Awareness

The question of awareness is one of time and space.

Our awareness is relative to the time of incidence and our spatial orientation.

The more we bring as individuals to awareness, the more we can glean.

Nature is the source we draw from to increase our awareness.

To be aware we are in the presence of a tree is simple awareness.

To know the tree's name, specie, history, and aura is increased awareness.

To be one with the tree in nature is full awareness.

The Unconscious

The most powerful of mental processes is the unconscious.

But what is it?

Where is the font?

Is it in past experience?

From a universal whole?

Does it stem cosmically from nature?

Is it all of the above and yet something else?

Like questions of theology,

We are just not sure.

My father used to call me unconscious.

I now believe that it was a complimentary term.

Wilderness

The salient word in wilderness is "wilder."

It is a wilder place or state of being.

It is untamed or unbridled.

Wilderness is beyond our comprehension.

Wilderness is the extra, the other, and the eternal.

John Muir taught us to love wilderness and not be afraid of it.

He gave us insight into the wilderness within us.

His love of pure wilderness is a model for us all.

All of the Best

Is the best yet to come?

What is the best?

The best is what we hardly ever think of.

A friend or lover does not get cancer.

A child is not hit by a speeding car.

A rare species of bird escapes a feral cat.

A leader of a foreign country looks after the interests of the poor.

A boy sitting all alone in his room figures out a way to be less depressed.

A little girl's horse decides not to buck.

Our old dog recovers from an illness.

Our local school hires a gifted teacher.

An artist completes a masterpiece.

An electorate pushes aside attempts to buy their votes and judges a leader fairly.

An American president decides to create a national monument.

In a little school, twenty healthy, little children put their hands over their hearts and pledge allegiance to the flag of the United States of America.

The best is yet to come.

The Pool of Love

The pool of love is a public pool.

We try to keep love private,

But the pool is always public.

To accommodate the love of the whole world, it must be large.

Most watch lovers in the pool with disdain.

The pool is generous.

It always grants power to the lovers.

Skilful lovers follow the tides governed by the moon.

They keep rhythm with the waves as they lap upon the shore.

The pool of love is the ocean.

We must take care of our ocean,

Or lose our pool of love.

Poetry

Now I have my tool box for poetry.

Metaphors, similes, analogies, and rhyme.

With these tools I can enter my subconscious mind.

I can spin the metaphor, play with similes, use analogies and rhyme.

I can express multiphase ideas with just a few words.

I can say exactly what I want to say.

I can express levels of meaning.

I can move through time.

I can change my place.

I can use words to form equations.

I can free my soul every day.

Evolution or Creation

Everything evolves.

I am not the same today as yesterday.

I have evolved and so have you.

Evolution is an undeniable reality.

Species evolve.

Evolution requires a time line.

Creation does not.

So when we argue about creation versus evolution,

We are arguing about time.

If linear time and eternity are simultaneous,

Creation exists within evolution.

So if we replace the "or" with "and,"

We have evolving creation.

Or we could simply say,

The evolution of creation.

The Company Lawyer

The first time he looked out the picture window,

He saw the beautiful scenery of Yosemite.

The bar of justice in Yosemite was easy to approach.

The degree of difficulty in facing the informal bar of justice in Yosemite

Was like trying to catch trout in a fish farm.

But then it happened.

The raging fires that closed the park,

The flood that within hours, destroyed campgrounds,

One-half of Yosemite Lodge, the sewer system, and roads.

Rock falls that killed in an instant.

Weighing life and death results in disciplinary actions.

Little by little the company lawyer realized that there was another bar of justice in Yosemite.

And now, when he looks out of his picture window, he sees it;

There, in the branches of the elm and the meadow grass;

There, in the waterfalls and cliffs;

There, on the wings of the raven.

Out there beyond the window glass is the nature bar of justice.

He doesn't talk about it,

But he is learning to practice before the nature bar.

Now he always feels like a beginner.

And being the only lawyer in town is terrifying.

Out there beyond the window glass,

Lives the deer mouse.

Of all things to be afraid of,

A mouse!

But, that little mouse carries the hantavirus.

Light and Shadow

The sunlight defines the Grizzly Giant, meadow grass and the monarch's wings.

When the clouds diffuse the light, the colors are stronger.

The impressionist's brush adds the white light to the color.

The transcendentalist's brush adds something else.

Between the shadows and the light,

There is a mysterious something else

Just beyond what can be perceived by the senses.

There, in the leaves of the giant sequoia,

Or there, in the leaves of the quaking aspen,

In the dim light, where forms start to lose their shape,

On the other side of that tree in the shade,

Under the wings of the raven,

In the occult other side just beyond our grasp,

A different light, an eternal light,

A different shadow, an eternal shadow,

Beyond the light and shadow we know,

Another light.

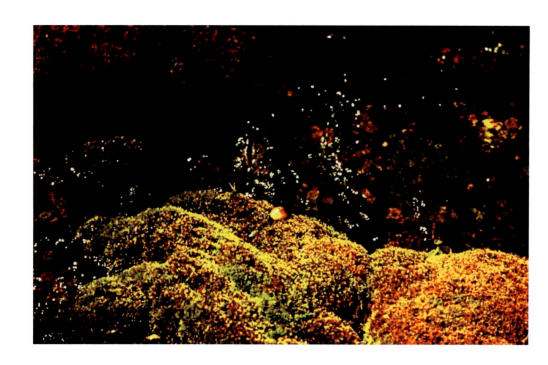

Nymphs, Fairies, Elves, Leprechauns, Sprites

In the braided creek of Bridal Veil Falls,

There where the water gurgles between the ferns,

Between the dogwood bushes,

Under the moss,

When the foggy mist rises,

They are there.

The fairies, leprechauns and elves are on the ferns and toadstools.

The sprites, and nymphs are in the water.

Creatures we can see only in our minds.

They dance and play in the moonlight.

They sing with the music of the brook.

They never tire because they are always part and parcel of the dancing light in the water.

If only we could share in their eternal joy and love of nature.

Meadow

Where it all began.

There is the source of life.

There the oxygen we breathe is made.

There the water we drink is stored and purified.

There the animals are given life.

The green permeates our soul.

The freshness gives us life.

The flowers, beauty.

The fine wetland filter is there.

The complex molecular filter that gives us intelligence.

The hope for our future.

The diversity that keeps us from going crazy.

Freedom.

The water gurgles.

The bubbles float to the surface.

The microbes dance and play.

The dance that gives us life.

Speaking Up for the Dead

The dead can no longer defend themselves.

We must defend them.

We live on their bones

We are supported by their lives.

The ones we remember and revere could see our time.

They fought for our freedom.

They defended our environment.

While we were yet unborn, they took care of our business.

When we were yet unborn, they acted bravely as if we were there.

They defended us!

It was as if we were the sleeping babies while they drove the car.

Through the dark and rainy night they drove, always vigilant.

In the end, they took us out of our baby seat,

Carried us into the house and tucked us into our crib.

While we slept, they watched and cared.

Now they sleep, and we must watch, care, and defend them.

Poet Paul Rivers, Circa 1972

The Poet Paul Rivers

He stood tall and distinguished looking in his Abraham Lincoln-style black top hat and worn, black clothes.

The first time I saw him, in 1972, he was a new hire working the freight dock.

Few men have stayed in my memories like Paul Rivers.

I asked him, "Paul, why do you always dress in black?"

With his deep, soft voice, he answered, "It's because I am against the Vietnam War.

With my black clothes, I mourn those who have died."

One night a bully had the forklift operator move a household box between the dock office and Paul so he could give Paul a beating.

I saw Paul's large hands turn to fists as he faced that bully.

Those black poet's hands told a story of hard work and more than one fight.

As soon as his eyes turned dark and he doubled his fists,

You could tell where this confrontation was going.

Paul went on to use his poet's hands to teach a bully a lesson.

He wasn't proud of his prowess at fighting;

He was proud of his poetry.

One day Paul said, "Bill, I want to read you my poem."

Paul stood there and calmly read his poem "Turn, Turn, and Turn."

Standing there at the back of his freight van,

Reading the lines to his poem about the way everything in Nature has its turn.

His turn had come to become a poet!

Writer

I really didn't start writing until I was 67.

I kept asking myself, "Now that you are writing, why do you feel so guilty?"

Whenever I started to write, I felt as if I had done something wrong and should feel guilty.

And yes, I still do, but now I know why.

It is the cries of those who have been dragged from their homes in the middle of the night and never seen again.

It is the pain and anguish of people being tortured and burned at the stake.

It is that young soldier who died face down in his own blood on the shore of Iwo Jima.

When I can write freely without fear because of them,

I feel guilty.

I ask myself, "Are you worthy to be called a writer?"

Trees

They give us air, water, food, shelter, industry, medicine, and solace for our souls.

They are our parents.

We and our children are their children,

If we don't take care of our parents,

There will be no future for us children.

Efficiency

Durability and efficiency are related.

The more efficient a plant, the longer it lives.

The oldest of trees are the most efficient.

When energy is conserved, efficiency increases.

Durability requires efficiency in the storage of energy.

Humans have become the least efficient of animals.

In nature the lack of the ability to hold energy spells a short life.

We stand out from other living creatures

In our multifarious ability to unlock, use, and waste stored energy.

Our ability to tap stored energy sources in complex ways

 Allows us to waste amazing amounts of energy.

The question for our children is,

How will they be required to account for our waste?

Light

Is it transitory illumination or is it something else?

If we could get ahead of its velocity, we could literally see the past.

We could see the dinosaurs and Julius Caesar address the Roman Senate,

Does light contain the potential of time atonement?

Light is equality.

It illuminates all in its path without discrimination.

The butterfly wing, the coyote's fur, the trout as it swims,

It illuminates all without charge.

Are there species of light?

Light beyond the light,

Light that illuminates our dreams,

Light of revelation,

Love's Light,

The light of genius and invention,

A nature's light.

Photograph by William Fontana Jr., Alaska 2012

Flight of the Eagle

From the high perch, she kicks loose,

Spreads her magnificent wings and soars.

Her eyes see the wild world in unbelievable clarity.

She sees each leaf, branch, and twig.

She sees the rabbit hop.

She sees the trout swim.

She can feel the humidity in the air.

She can hear the mouse in the field.

She can smell the freshly made oxygen.

She tastes the sacrament of the wild in her prey.

To go hither and yon, she only needs to will it so.

She can land where no other living thing has touched.

She is subject to nothing other than her craft.

What exhilaration!

What pure joy to fly with no constraint,

To hear the sound of the wind rushing by her feathers as she dives.

To be assured that she can never fall.

She will always soar freely in the wild.

She will never be subjected to any will but her own.

The wilderness was created for her,

For her moment, for her reality, and for her beauty.

And she is constantly assured

It will remain in her talons forever.

Field Mouse

Among the smallest of mammals,

Pound for pound the most amazing.

Hunted or hated by most of the animal kingdom.

They must be extremely fast.

They can outrun a coyote in a short distance.

Every step must be an irretrievable step of faith.

There are no wings to give them a second chance.

To err is to die.

They must be the quickest and most accurate.

In their burrow, they love, take care of their young, and hide from the world.

Embarrassingly they are so much like us.

And yet, in some ways superior.

Master Fisherman
Ron Silva (Ras)

When we met,

It did not matter,

If it was the first time

Or the last.

His spirit was always the same,

Friendly, educational, and helpful,

A mechanic by trade.

We talked about fishing.

Ras talked about catching trout, salmon, and bass.

He told me about fishing the Merced River, ranch ponds, and lakes.

In a moment his story could transport you

To a secluded fishing hole in Costa Rica

I traveled many times through his stories.

I was there with him when his cast

Placed the fly on the water,

When the fish struck

For the contest,

 For the gentle live release

Of the fish back into the water,

A wonderful story told by a master fisherman.

All told, over the years his stories revealed

The world of a master fisherman.

Extra awareness of the environment,

And the cool, soft power of the water,

The importance of tracking all of the elements of nature,

Changing weather and atmospheric conditions,

Sounds and scents,

Types of plants and insects around the fishing hole.

The mayfly, mosquito, dragonfly, and hellgrammite,

His own hand tied-flies around a barbless hook,

Fishing in harmony with nature,

Love of fish.

Their color and their spirit

And their passion for life.

Please, Master Ras,

Just one more cast!

Transparency

Light in its multifarious forms makes transparency.

But, what is light?

The light of the sun?

The light of life?

Is it the light of the soul?

In a leaf, the transparent mixture of reflected sunlight and absorbed light.

In the animal, the blending of the wild specie dimension that they belong to
And their own memories.

In a human, the blending of experience and passion.

Transparency is the in between-overlapping mixture,

In which we can discover mysterious tertiary qualities

Light and dark,

Present and past,

Life and death,

Future, and Infinite.

We look for meaning in the overlapping transparencies.

We find only mystery,

But we must keep looking,

For, there are meanings

In the transparencies.

POLITY

Support.

Military, political, religious, personal.

Always an incomprehensible mixture.

What does any given mixture of power mean?

When we make a political decision,

What are the consequences?

What about appeal?

Animal polity is in nature.

We opine that human polity

Can be separated from nature.

For support in the polity of nature,

We must consider the cosmic currents.

The currents that can only be felt by intuition.

They have nothing to do with convention.

Their push and pull are ultimate power.

Spinning and Weaving

We are made up of various odds and ends from nature.

Water, air, fire, and earth.

A leaf, a feather, a piece of old cloth.

We have lost all account of what makes us up.

There are too many things and all too desperate.

The spinning has homogenized us.

We are spun singularly and as a group.

When we are born we are fully together.

Our fabric is woven so tightly

It takes us a long time to unravel.

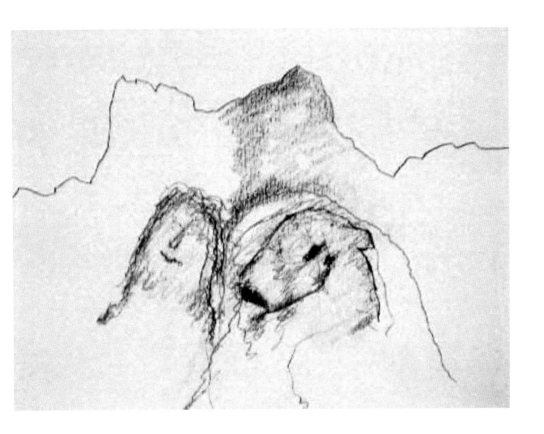

Calculations

When we are yet babies, we start our calculations.

We learn to gauge the distance to the chair or door.

Our mind forms the math of the universe.

We start to unlock the secrets of our surroundings.

The math is more complex

Than we could ever consciously understand.

Quickly we test our calculations to see if they work.

When they fail, we recalculate and form a new mathematical model.

We learn to trust our internal calculator.

In my relationship to nature, I have formed my calculations.

I have been forced to recalculate many times.

And now I know all of my calculations are wrong.

I could fall back on sensual information,

But I am sure that those calculations would fail in the proof.

Love

For there to be love,

One must like.

Like is the most important part of love.

After passion dies,

One must ask,

Do I like?

In the world of love,

The only reason to love is to like.

If one loves for gain or power,

Like eludes them.

It's very simple,

If you want love

All that is necessary,

Is to like.

Rainbow

The mystery of color is in the rainbow,

What glory of color in sequence!

Transitory and yet eternal.

Our emotions vary as their colors divide,

We can feel the magic of their colors,

In them can be seen the glory of the hereafter.

Rainbows are the constant of the universe.

In the expanse of the universe,

We cannot see beyond the rainbow.

Snow

White and fluffy,

Silent and crystalline.

Life itself is falling from the sky.

Hope for the salamanders.

Love itself is fluttering down.

What joy springs with the sight of snow.

Our planet will still support our life and reality,

As long as we can see snow.

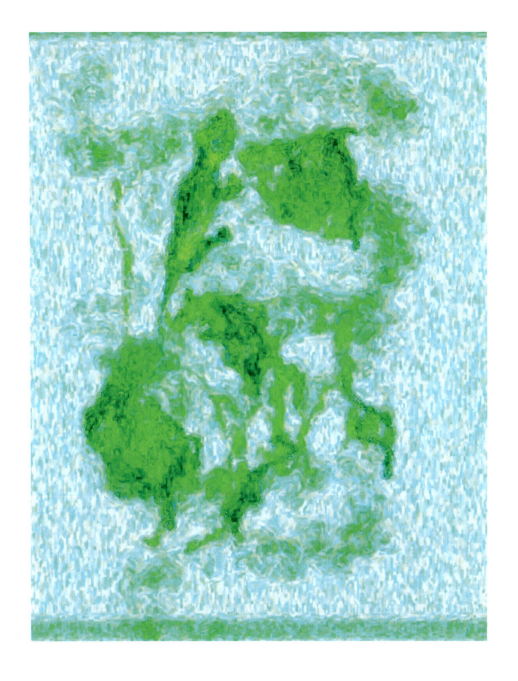

Salamander

In your pristine water world,

Only the purest and most vibrantly verdant, wild world will do.

All of the things that will kill us slowly will kill you quickly.

You are so fragile and yet so beautiful.

Even if we touch you,

You will be harmed.

You represent more than an aquatic animal.

You represent what we have lost.

You used to be able to live everywhere,

But now, there are few places left for you.

We want to somehow reach out and touch your sparkling clean aquatic world.

If only we had the power to save you,

We might be able to save ourselves.

Fox

We admire you!

Your fur is so beautiful,

Your tail so magnificent.

You live by the night.

There are no restrictions for you.

You are absolutely wild and free.

When we chase you with horses and hounds,

We are trying to capture your freedom and spirit.

Your spent body does not give us what we seek.

A million fox hunts could not give us any part of what you have.

Unlike us,

You will always be free!

Mountain Lion

Master of the night,

Hunter and fighter,

Are you still the king of the forest?

Do you know how important you are to us?

Without you we become unbalanced.

You take your prey animals without side effects.

We cannot do that.

We are forced to waste but you are not.

Your craft is narrow, pure, and blameless.

You are a straightforward animal without pretense.

We could never face you in a fair fight.

What joy can there be in killing you

By cheating?

Image by William Fontana Jr., 2014

Lone Wolf

You have traveled a great distance to escape;

We have killed your family.

How lonely you must be!

We have taken not only your family

But also your home the wilderness.

Your grief goes unnoticed by us.

When you fight back,

We only hate you more.

And yet when you die,

Something within us,

Also dies.

Photograph from author's collection, Main St., Livermore, Ca. Circa 1972

Dream

There you are, just as before,

You are lovely and precious.

I kiss you and hold you,

Then I realize that I have lost my car.

Where did I park it?

Was it on this street or the one before?

I can't be sure.

I start to look for my car

And find myself among people

I have never seen before.

Then someone asks me for directions to the fair.

Suddenly I am by a Ferris wheel looking for my son.

I can't find him.

I feel all alone and insignificant,

Just another face,

Lost in the crowd.

Resurrection

I was resurrected today.

A part of me that had died was brought back to life.

Resurrection is an ongoing thing.

Each night we die in the land of dreams,

Only to be resurrected in the morning.

The little boy or girl that we were,

Is resurrected,

If only to play,

For a little while.

How many stages in development have we all gone through?

How many personalities do we have?

Were they cancelled when completed or unused?

They are resurrected as we go.

Resurrection surrounds us, embraces us,

And we don't even know it.

We talk about a final resurrection,

But that can't be!

Resurrection is constant,

Resurrection can't be final,

Resurrection is life!

NGC 2237 Rosette Nebula photograph by Ted Wolfe

Cosmos

We are of the warp and weave of the cosmos.

We are made of water from the comets.

In the still of the night, we see the stars that gave us birth.

The astrologers have connected us to the heavens emotionally.

The astronomers have connected us to the heavens scientifically.

Beyond astrology and astronomy,

We are birthed that way.

We come from out there.

We will return to out there.

In our dreams we visit the font of our birth.

When awake, we walk the extension of our birth.

When resurrected, we celebrate the eternity and promise of the heavens.

Positive Change

In the constant of the universe,

Change has three forms,

Active, passive, and that which is beyond our sensual perception,

In nature, we see the craft-wise combination of the active and the passive in change

In the bird learning to fly and the caterpillar becoming a butterfly,

Directed change is most varied in humanity.

We can choose and direct our individual change.

We can choose the nature and source of our change.

We can direct ourselves to be a poet, or a fool, or both.

Metaphysical change remains our greatest mystery.

What is the nature of change in death?

From the pure beauty we see in the heavens,

We can be assured

Of the great constant,

And we can believe in the durability of glory.

The great moments and achievements of individuals slip by,

Plateau by plateau,

A child learns to walk, talk, run and ski,

A president becomes Abraham Lincoln,

A poet becomes William Shakespeare,

The transient glory in individual plateaus

Passed by in the slipstream of time,

Individual plateaus mostly lost

Recorded only in our

Individual memories.

But are they lost?

I think not, glorious levels of achievement all add to the celestial music.

Remembered in every detail,

They become the eternal font of future transition,

So that we can be assured,

Whatever wonderful plateau of excellence

Once reached in nature,

Is always there

And will always be there.

Adding the glory of the beauty we see in the heavens.

Layers

Buried under layers of repression.

Billy, the knife and spoon go on the right,

The fork on the left.

Comb your hair, Billy.

Billy you have to stay back in the second grade.

It wasn't until I started writing these poems that I realized how much my soul had been buried under repression.

Once I became free to make my metaphors and to explain my insights, I realized that my soul had found an escape from the layers.

Layer upon layer gone with the touch of a key.

Free at last to play!

IMAGE CREDITS

The images that accompany the poems are the artwork of William Fontana Sr.   http://fontana-art.com/ with the following exceptions:

The photograph of the bald eagle that accompanies the poem "Flight of the Eagle," and the drawing that accompanies the poem "Lone Wolf" are both works of William Fontana Jr. http://willsview.com/

The poem "Rite of the Sword" is accompanied by a edited (slightly cropped) version of "Death of Barbararadziwill" by Józef Simmler (1823–1868) obtained from http://en.wikipedia.org/wiki/Barbara_Radziwi%C5%82%C5%82

The image "NGC 2237: - Color" that accompanies the poem "Cosmos," is obtained from Ted Wolfe (tedwolfe.com) and is from his gallery of amazing celestial photographs. "NGC 2237: Rosette Nebula" was used with the permission of Ted Wolfe. It was provided to the author by Ted Wolfe from his fantastic collection of celestial photographs that can be seen on his website: http://www.tedwolfe.com/

Made in the USA
Middletown, DE
06 December 2023